The Story of Capta with the Hum

George Wharton James

Alpha Editions

This edition published in 2024

ISBN : 9789362924445

Design and Setting By
Alpha Editions
www.alphaedis.com
Email - info@alphaedis.com

As per information held with us this book is in Public Domain.
This book is a reproduction of an important historical work. Alpha Editions uses the best technology to reproduce historical work in the same manner it was first published to preserve its original nature. Any marks or number seen are left intentionally to preserve its true form.

Contents

INTRODUCTION .... - 1 -

CAPTAIN'S OWN STORY .... - 11 -

HOW I BOUGHT AND TRAINED
CAPTAIN *By His Owner*, W. A. SIGSBEE .... - 25 -

A SCIENTIFIC INVESTIGATION .... - 37 -

CAPTAIN'S PRAYER OF
THANKSGIVING .... - 45 -

INTRODUCTION

Early in the year 1915 I was called to lecture on California and the West in the beautiful Sunset Theater of the Southern Pacific Building at the San Francisco Exposition. In taking a survey of the *Zone* I was soon attracted to a gigantic horse in process of manufacture out of wood and plaster, and a placard before it indicated that a trained horse would soon be shown here. Being fond of animals, naturally, and having seen and read considerably of trained horses, I was ready for the first opening of this show, and there was introduced to CAPTAIN, the educated horse, or, as he has been termed, "the horse with the human brain." My opinions as to the quality of Captain's intelligence I have recorded later, but his first performance was a delight to me. His appearance was pleasing. He looked well cared for, contented, happy and willing to go through his exhibition. There was none of the holding back, the whipping, the sharp orders, the ugly looks one so generally sees on the faces of "trained animals" when they are being put through their tricks. Most of these poor creatures show so manifestly that they are trapped, are made to do what they do not like, and that they resent it, that I seldom can tolerate the sight of their anger and humiliation—for that is clearly what nearly every animal reveals to me at these exhibitions. Here, on the other hand, was an animal that enjoyed his work. He treated it as fun; just as my own Arab colt treats a free run and then being led into his corral and being petted. After a little pleasantry his master asked him to count the number of ladies on the front row. Captain's eyes at once began at one end, followed the row, down to the other end, and, by pawing, he told the number. Several similar questions were asked, as, for instance, how many gentlemen in the second row; how many women along the aisle; how many girls, or boys, in the second or third rows, etc., and in every case Captain gave the answer correctly.

Then a standard was brought forward containing numbers, to which were attached leather lugs or holders. These were held in the standard, or rack, and placed without any relative order, and scores of later observations, have convinced me that there is no order in which they can be placed that makes any difference to Captain. Here he showed his familiarity with numbers, bringing from the rack any one called for. Then tests in arithmetic were applied, such as the addition of numbers as 9 plus 6 plus 7. Captain at once picked out the figure 2 and then after dropping it, picked it up and showed it again. Subtraction was equally well performed, and multiplication up to 12 times 12, and the answers given were invariably correct.

In giving the answers he pawed with one of his front feet, but at the request of his master would give a portion of the answer with one foot, and the remainder with another, even alternating in his use of his hind feet.

A number of simple commands were now given, and questions asked to which the horse responded with a shake of the head for No, or a nod for Yes. He would take a seat when requested, scratch his head with right or left hindfoot, show either right or left foot when required, or stamp with right or left foot when required, or stamp with right or left hindfoot as asked. When told to pump water he would swing his head up and down continuously, and he would swing his head to right and left as commanded. When asked to laugh he opened his mouth and showed his teeth, and he wiggled his ears with equal readiness. When told to put out his tongue it came out immediately, and when commanded to make a hobby-horse of himself he planted his hindfeet firmly and then proceeded to stretch himself by planting his forefeet as far ahead as he could.

He was then required to make a corkscrew of himself, and placing all four feet together, moved around in corkscrew motion. At the command: "Reverse!" he immediately went in the opposite direction.

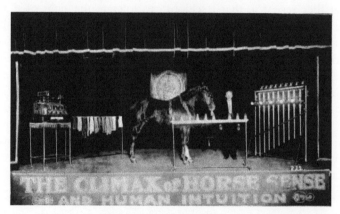

Captain on the stage with his trainer and owner,
Captain W. A. Sigsbee. Cash register and colored cloth rack to the left; number rack and chimes to the right.

Madame Ellis in one of her wonderful mind reading performances at the San Diego Exposition, where she exhibited daily with Captain.

Then came an exhibition of Captain's recognition of colors. A rack containing ten or fifteen colored cloths was placed before the audience. The horse was asked to go and pick out, say, the third lady in the second row, look at the color of her hat (or shawl, dress, gloves or other article of apparel), and then take up the cloth from the rack which corresponded to the color of the article worn. In this he seldom made mistakes.

Now a blindfold exhibition was given. As his master explained, this fully precluded the possibility of any collusion—at least as far as Captain's *seeing* any signal was concerned. The blindfold was a leather mask, held in place by the ears and a supporting and fastening strap, the leather completely covering the eyes.

All the various commands of "Pump," "Wiggle your ears," "Laugh," "Put out your tongue," "Corkscrew," "Say Yes!" "No!" were given and immediately and correctly responded to. Then Captain was asked to bite his right knee, lift up his left foot, scratch his head with his rear left, or right foot, etc.

Numbers were now called for, addition, subtraction and multiplication required, and the answers beaten out, or pawed, with whatever foot was suggested.

Then his memory was tested. A red cloth was tied to his right foreknee, and a white one on his left hind leg. As the tying was done his master carefully cautioned him not to forget. Now for a few minutes, he was kept occupied with numbers, and then was asked for the white cloth, afterwards for the red one. In both cases he gave whichever was called for. But it should be noted that in neither case did Mr. Sigsbee give him the command. Someone in the audience was asked to call for whichever colored cloth he desired, and on several occasions I made the request myself. The blindfold was now removed.

The exhibition with the Cash Register then followed, Captain being asked to get a paper dollar, then change it for small silver, when he brought out half a dollar and two quarters. There were many variations of the use of money to all of which requests he responded with accuracy.

Then he was called to the chimes and the audience was informed that Captain could play "Nearer, My God to Thee," or "The Suwanee River," and it could make its choice. The former tune was called for and Captain played it correctly, as far as the notes were concerned, though the time was not, indeed could not have been, followed, as the clapper was moved by an upward thrust of the horse's nose upon a lever.

These, in the main, were his achievements. They delighted, yet, at the same time, puzzled me. How did he accomplish them? By the kindness of his owner, Mr. W. A. Sigsbee, I was permitted to visit Captain in his stall as often as I chose. As I got to know him better my interest increased, until I decided that I should like to write his story. After talking the matter over with Mr. Sigsbee, he was quite willing, but, somehow, my year in San Francisco was so crowded that the great Exposition closed without this pleasing task being accomplished.

The following year we met again, however, at the Panama-California International Exposition, in San Diego, and there I seized the time necessary to write the following story.

While I cannot say with Homer Davenport that I have been so profoundly interested in horses that at three years and nine months old I drew illustrations of Arab horses, I can say with truth that I have always been interested in any animal that showed any approach to what is generally regarded as human intelligence. I was born and brought up as a good Methodist. God, to me, was the Creator of all things, and however my belief in other matters of religion may have been modified or altered, in that particular I believe as I have ever believed. If, then, God is the Creator of all things, animate and inanimate, every creature high or low, is a manifestation of His thought, His care, His love, *and all are born—created—of the same Spirit, and therefore, are akin.* To me this is a truth more powerful than mere logic can ever make it. There is a Spirit within me—of the Creator, undoubtedly—that bears witness to this truth. Hence I know no difference between the spirit in the horse and that in the man, except in the degree of its outward manifestation. However, my good friend, John Burroughs, writes:

We know that the animals do not think in any proper sense as we do, or have concepts and ideas, because they have no language. Thinking in any proper sense is impossible without language; the language is the concept. Our ideas are as inseparable from the words as form is from substance. We may have impressions, perceptions, emotions, without language, but not ideas. The child perceives things, discriminates things, knows its mother from a stranger, is angry, or glad, or afraid, long before it has any language or any proper concepts. Animals know only things through their senses, and this "Knowledge is restricted to things present in time and space." Reflection, or a return upon themselves in thought,—of this they are not capable. Their only language consists of various cries and calls, expressions of pain, alarm, joy, love, anger. They communicate with each other and come to share each other's mental or emotional states, through these cries and calls. A dog barks in various tones also, each of which expresses a different feeling in the dog. . . . The lowing and bellowing of horned cattle are expressions of several different things. The crow has many caws, that no doubt convey various meanings. The cries of alarm and distress of the birds are understood by all the wild creatures that hear them; a feeling of alarm is conveyed to them—an emotion, not an idea. We evolve ideas from our emotions, and emotions are often begotten by our ideas. A fine spring morning or a prospect from a mountain top makes one glad, and this gladness may take an intellectual form. But without language this gladness could not take form in ideal concepts. . . . We have only to think of the animals as habitually in a condition analogous to or identical with the unthinking and involuntary character of much of our lives. They are creatures of routine. They are wholly immersed in the unconscious, involuntary nature out of which we rise, and above which our higher lives go on.[1]

This logic seems complete and unassailable. Yet, nevertheless, there is within me something that is not satisfied. I grant Burroughs the argument, and then fall back upon my own inner consciousness with reasoning somewhat after this line: We do not now know the language of the animals; we do not know whether they have one or not. Their lives *seem* imprisoned within the dark pent-house of brute-life where no gleam of our kind of intellectual light reaches them. But may it not be that they feel this imprisonment and are striving to escape from it. The Indians have many legends that speak of a time when gods, men, animals and all nature had a common tongue. May this not be true, or if not true of the past, a vision of the natural outgrowth of the future? If God be the Creator He must comprehend all His creation. As we approximate nearer to Him—and Browning asserts we are all gods, though in the germ—may we not begin to understand more fully the languageless animals?

Our acceptance of the Hebraic Law as set forth in the Old Testament has made us look upon the animals as created solely for our benefit, ours to use just as we choose. Unfortunately this power to *use* has given to those with small modicum of kindness in their disposition the feeling that they are also within their manly rights to *misuse* the animals. Considering the greatness of the Universe and the finiteness of man as compared with the whole, does not this idea seem preposterous?

The Buddhist and Hindu religions teach that all life is *One*—that on its journey from unconsciousness to self-consciousness it passes through all the kingdoms of nature,—mineral, vegetable, molluscar, reptilian, bird, animal, human, up to superhuman. They say about this *life* that "it *sleeps* in the mineral, *dreams* in the flowers, *awakens* in the animal, and *becomes active* in the human." Hence the Hindu treats the animals as his *younger brothers*, and the slaughter and abuse of them tolerated and practiced in the West is practically unknown in the East, except where the so-called Western civilization has intruded. This view, too, would transcend the arguments and logic of Burroughs.

Then, too, may it not be our privilege to *help* the animals escape from their dark prison cell into the light of mental exercise? I see no reason why animals should not evolve, ascend in the scale, and develop language, reason, concepts, ideas, as well as man. It is certainly going to do no harm to believe it possible, to hope for it, and to *work for it*. Love is a great revelator in many ways, and the love of man, intelligently exercised in relationship to animals, may be of wonderful help in opening the door of their brute prison-houses.

Hence, I hail every effort, whether of child with its pet, shepherd with his dog, woman with her parrot, or educated scholar with his horses, to *find the way* that shall help the animal know his kinship with the human. Too long have we assumed that there was no crossing the gulf between the animal and the human. Man's *assumptions* have shut knowledge away from him. Instead of "assuming" that the horse had no intelligence why did he not go to work scientifically to find out what he did have? Just as Sir John Lubbock experimented with all kinds of creatures as to their powers of taste, smell, touch, etc., only in a larger and higher way, man might have tested the intelligence of horses, and then sought to improve it.

There is too much assumption in human beings about most things,—animal instinct and human reason not excluded. What I wish to protest against, with emphasis and vigor, is the assumption that we know all there is to know about intelligence—that we know the limits Nature herself has placed upon its development, and that all efforts to foster further development are useless. I affirm that we do *not* know; that we have never, as yet, even tried to know; and that until men with loving, devoted, sympathetic singleness of heart and purpose seek to develop *all there is* in the mentality of all the lower animals,—dogs, cats, deer, as well as horses,—shall we begin to have a *real* foundation for our assumptions upon the subject.

I am still simple enough to believe implicitly in the Spiritual Controller of the Universe we call God. I am still enamoured of the belief that as Browning says in "Saul"

> God made all the creatures and gave them our love and
> our fear,
>
> To give sign, we and they are His children, one family
> here.

Romanes claims for the horse an intelligence less than that of the larger carnivora, the elephant, or even the ass. Yet he asserts that the emotional life of the horse is remarkable, and that working through the emotions wonderful results of training have been secured. He says it is an affectionate animal, pleased at being petted, jealous of companions receiving favor, greatly enjoying play with others of its kind, and thoroughly entering into the sport of the hunting-field. Horses also exhibit pride in a marked degree, as also do mules, being unmistakably pleased with gay trappings.

Now is it inconceivable that these animals might some day, somehow, find a door open whereby they could enter into the realm of speech. To *feel* is certainly a large step towards *expression*, and to my mind, the possession of the one power suggests the *close proximity* of the other.

I read with great interest the arguments—as different from the mere assumptions—of those who assert that the instinct of animals, and the reason of human beings, are two separate and distinct things; there is a deep gulf between them which can never be passed by the lower order. I do not believe this. Rather do I hold with Romanes that:

> No distinct line can be drawn between instinct and reason. Whether we look to the growing child or to the ascending scale of animal life, we find that instinct shades into reason by imperceptible degrees.

Instinct certainly involves some kind of mental operations, and by this feature it is clearly distinguished and differentiated from reflex action. One bold difference between instinct and reason, I contend, is that the actions of instinct are uniform, though performed by different individuals of the same species, while reason—however limited in its operations—leads to the performance of individualistic actions, limited to single personalities. Instinct implies "mental action directed towards the accomplishment of adaptive movement, antecedent to individual experience, without necessary knowledge of the relation between the means employed and the ends attained, but similarly performed under the same appropriate circumstances by all the individuals of the same species."[2]

In all these particulars instinct differs from reason, in that it, "besides involving a mental constituent, and besides being concerned in adaptive action, is always *subsequent* to individual experience, never acts but upon a definite and often laboriously acquired knowledge of the relation between means and ends, and is very far from being always similarly performed under the same appropriate circumstances by all the individuals of the same species."[3]

Where there is an intentional adaptation of means to ends there is clear indication of reason. This adaptation I claim Captain possesses, as distinctively, though of course on a much lower plane than I myself possess it. For instance: When Captain, *of his own volition*, after finding his groom asleep after being awakened, went to him again and pulled the covers from his bed, that may have been accident the first time. It led to the groom's awakening, arising and feeding the horse. Now was it not conscious adaptation of means to that end when, the next morning, on the groom, failing to arise and feed him, Captain deliberately went and pulled the bed clothes from him, and has done it ever since?

Romanes, in his *Animal Intelligence*, clearly suggests the processes by which we may study or investigate the operations of animal intelligence. Says he:

> If we contemplate our own mind, we have an immediate cognizance of a certain flow of thoughts or feelings, which are the most ultimate things, and indeed the only things, of which we are cognizant.... But in our objective analysis of other or foreign minds we have no such immediate cognizance; all our knowledge of their operations is derived, as it were, through the medium of ambassadors—these ambassadors being the activities of the organism.... Starting from what I know subjectively of the operation of my own individual mind, and the activities which in my own organism they prompt, I proceed

by analogy to infer from the observable activities of other organisms what are the mental operations that underlie them.[4]

Upon any hypothesis of the development of human or animal intelligence it is evident that mentality is of a wonderfully varied quality. There is a distinct, though by no means clearly defined, sliding scale of intelligence. It is universal knowledge that a dog shows more intelligence than a frog, and a horse than a turtle; and human intelligences are as widely separated as the Igorrote and a Hottentot and a Gladstone or a Tagore. Where the horse's place is, in the sliding scale of general intelligence, I do not know; nor can I tell exactly where Captain should be located in the varying scale of the intelligence of horses in general. But this I do know. He has intelligence, and it is much superior to that commonly shown by the majority of horses. And I firmly believe with Captain Sigsbee that training and discipline have their effect in bringing up the intelligence of the higher order of horses to the intelligence of the lower class, or child, level of humans.

I am decidedly opposed to the assumption that the intelligence of horses is a fixed and immovable mental quantity; that no amount of kindly, sympathetic, and understanding training by thoughtful men, will add to, or develop what they already possess. I believe, beyond the power of any logical formula to shake my belief, that any constant contact of the soul of man with whatever there is in horses that corresponds to the soul must produce a resulting awakening, quickening, deepening of that soul—something in both man and animal.

It is in this light, therefore, that what I write of Captain's "human intelligence" must be understood. He is developing. He has awakened, so far. He has begun the upward journey. The more he is "educated" the nearer the true resemblance to human intelligence will he display.

If, in any way, these pages help forward the day of closer sympathy between man and his lesser or younger brothers and sisters, I shall be amply repaid for the labor of writing them.

GEORGE WHARTON JAMES.

The Exposition, San Diego, Christmas, 1916.

---

[1] "Do Animals Think," Harper's Monthly, Vol. 110, p. 358.

[2] Romanes, pp.

5, 16.

[3] Romanes, p. 16.

[4] Animal Intelligence, by J. G. Romanes, p. 1. D. Appleton & Co., 1888.

CAPTAIN'S OWN STORY

I was born on June 8, 1905, on the farm of Judge J. H. Cartwright, in Oregon, Ill. My mother's name was *Robey*, and my father's, *Sidney*. While I was a little colt the Judge called me *Sid Bell*. He used to come to the barn and look me over and recount what he called my "points" to his friends, and when I was in the pasture running to and fro, kicking up my heels, and thoroughly enjoying myself, he would stand looking on, apparently thinking very hard. One day the groom tied me to my mother's side, and the Judge drove her out over the road, and he seemed very pleased at the way I trotted along. Day after day he did this, for a long time, making me go faster and faster until I heard him, and other people, say that I was going to be a very fast pacer. My lungs expanded with the exercise; my muscles grew strong and firm; my eyes were bright and clear; I had a hearty appetite and enjoyed every mouthful I ate, and every day when they turned me loose in the pasture, I raced up and down just as proud and happy and full of life and exuberant spirits as ever possessed a young horse in all the wide world.

One day the Judge took me out on what was called a "track." It was a smooth oval place, not very wide, arranged solely for the purpose of driving horses. They fastened a light little cart behind me, hardly big enough for my groom to sit in, and then he made me go around that track as hard as I could go. Of course he let me go easy at first, until I—what he called—"warmed up," and then he would say, "Now, Sid Bell. Go to it!" and would give that peculiar clicking sound that men make when they want a horse to hurry up, and I paced ahead as fast as I knew how.

The Judge used to come and watch proceedings nearly every day, and give suggestions to my groom. Some days he would be very proud and boastful about me, and other times, not quite so well satisfied. But one day, when I was feeling particularly good, and had gone around the track at a lively clip, I heard him say "He'll do! He made it that time in 2:16," which I afterwards learned meant that I had paced a mile in two minutes and sixteen seconds, and that was accounted pretty fast for a two-year-old colt.

When I was nearly three years old the Judge sold me to Mr. W. A. Sigsbee of Chicago. My mother had told me, one day when Mr. Sigsbee came to the track to watch me pace, that he was a great animal trainer, known all over the country as Captain Sigsbee. I heard the Captain say "He's a beauty. His action is fine," and when I was brought up to where he and the Judge were standing he repeated these and many other comments, all of a nature to make a young horse like me think a good deal of himself, so that I looked at him and let him know by my eyes that I liked him to speak in that way about me. Then he began to talk about my "intelligent look" and all at once he exclaimed, quite emphatically: "Judge, I've got to have that colt. I want to train him and make him the best known horse in the world." The Judge didn't seem to like this idea very much, at first. He said he had trained me for the track, and he didn't intend to part with me, but Captain Sigsbee urged so strongly that it would be far better for me, to keep me away from the track, and let me be especially trained and then sent out through the country as an educated horse, that finally he consented to sell me.

My mother was very sorry to have me go away from her, and I was sorry to go, but she seemed to find a great deal of comfort in the fact that I should no longer be on the track; I should have a much less strenuous life than racing, and that the education my new owner wished to give me would also be much to my advantage in other ways.

So Captain Sigsbee took me to Chicago. And my! what a noisy, bustling city it was. How different from the quiet country where I was born and so far had spent my life. And the smells! Why, I smelled more horrible smells in one day there, I think, than I had smelled in all my life before. The same with the noises. People think horses don't care about smells and noises. Don't they? I was jumping and nervous all the time with the new and awful noises that seemed to rush at me from every direction. Street cars, roaring, rushing and their bell clanging; automobiles honking right in my ears; wagons rumbling over the stones; men shouting; women and girls talking with high-pitched voices; babies squalling; policemen whistling at the street crossings; newsboys shouting their papers; beggars grinding away on their pitiful little organs; and a thousand other noises, many of which I had never before heard. As we were crossing one of the streets or avenues a new noise came rushing at me, as fast as an automobile travels, but it was over my head. I looked up, but could see nothing but trestle-work above me, and the noise was loud enough to be felt. Nearer it came, until with a rush and a roar, it seemed to fall on me, and I reared and struggled and even screamed in my terror. Then in a moment the fierce noise of it was gone, and it gradually grew less and less. But in another street I had the same experience. Captain spoke quietingly and soothingly to me and told me I needn't be scared as it was "only the elevated railway," but I didn't know then what he meant. Of course, I learned all about it later, and then I was no longer scared.

At the training-barn I had a fine large box-stall, the floor covered with clean, sweet-smelling hay, where I could lie down and rest whenever I felt like it. My new owner was very kind to me. He came to see me several times a day, and brought his friends, and told them how proud he was of me. He always brought me an apple, a carrot, a lump of sugar or something I liked, and I soon watched for his coming. I learned to love him. But I did not like being left alone in that strange place, and with so many disagreeable smells and noises around me. When he went away I tried to beg him not to go. I would "nose up" to him and even try to hold him, but he only called me "a cunning rascal," and broke away. Then I would whinny and paw and paw so that I was sure if he had any real horse-sense he would surely know what I meant, and that I was telling him so clearly that even a mule or a donkey would understand *that I did not want him to leave me alone*. But poor creature, he was only a man, and didn't have *horse-sense*, so I was left. When he came again I showed him by my gladness and the reality of my welcome how glad I was he had come.

One day while he was away some rude and noisy men got into a quarrel outside the stable, and they fought, and swore, and made an awful noise. One of them fired a gun or a revolver at the other, and the hubbub was terrible. I was dreadfully alarmed, and when the Captain came, a little while after, I was lathered all over with the sweat that had poured out of me because I was so afraid.

"My, my!" he exclaimed, as soon as he saw me, "this will never do. The poor little fellow's scared almost to death. I'll never leave him alone again."

How glad I was to hear that. I kissed him, just as I had learned to kiss my mother, and tried to show him my gratitude. He kept his word, and that very night he brought a groom to me, whom he called Chili. He told Chili he was never to leave me, day or night. He was to be my companion and caretaker. He must not try to teach me, or anything of that kind, but just simply see that I had plenty of hay and water and my oats regularly, and an abundance of litter to sleep on, that I was kept perfectly clean, my stable also clean and sweet, and be with me all the time. That was a great comfort to me. Few people can know how much, for I really believe, now that I am older, that horses are far more fearful and timid even than women and colts than babies. We are an awfully scary lot. It's too bad, but it is so!

By this time Captain Sigsbee had decided that I was going to suit his purpose perfectly, so he gave me his own name, that everybody might know I was his horse. He was known all over the country as Captain Sigsbee, and if I bore his name, hundreds of thousands of people would know, as soon as they heard it, who had trained me.

But he never called me "Captain" while he was visiting me in the stable; nor did he ever allow Chili to call me "Captain." I was always "Boy!" except when he was teaching me. You see there was a reason for that. When he said "Captain," I soon learned that we were at school and I must attend strictly to business; at other times I used to do as I liked, but when we began "work," I found out I had to take everything seriously, do just as I was told, and stick to my lessons, trying hard to learn what I was being taught. If I didn't I failed to get the carrots, apples, sugar or candy that I expected.

Chili used to sleep in the stall next to mine, and I was generally left free, and as there were no doors or bars I could go and see if he was there at any time, if I felt nervous or afraid. One morning he didn't get up to feed me at the usual time—6 a. m.—and I waited until I was pretty hungry. Then I decided to go and see what was the matter. He was still sound asleep, so I leaned my head over him and rubbed his face with my nose. That woke him up, right away, and he jumped up and fed me. He laughed and patted me and called me a cute fellow, and said I was a smart horse, so, when he failed to get up and feed me the next time, I didn't wait but went right up to his cot and did it again. I did this several times, and always got my feed right away, but one morning, after I woke Chili he must have dropped off to sleep again. When he didn't come with my oats I went around to see what the matter was and there he was sound asleep again, with the covers pulled up over his head. I felt a little bit angry with him for neglecting me like that, so I just took hold of the bed-clothes, gave them a yank, and pulled them right down nearly to the foot of the cot.

My! my! how he jumped! He was out of that cot in a flash,—but he laughed and said there was no beating me, he'd have to give up. I hardly knew just what he meant at the time, but I had learned a good lesson, for ever since then I don't waste any time in waking my groom, and if he doesn't bring me my feed on time I go and pull off the bed-clothes from him, and I get my oats without further delay, even though sometimes, after giving me my breakfast he goes back again to bed and takes another snooze. Chili and I soon became good friends, but that did not take away my affection for my master. I was always glad to see him. He used to come and talk to me—man talk, of course—but I soon learned to know a great deal of what he said, and I always paid attention—well, perhaps, to be strictly truthful I would better say nearly always—for he never failed, when I did so, to give me some tidbit or other that I much enjoyed. Of all these I liked sugar the best, but he says too much sugar isn't good for me, so I never get quite as much as I would like.

During all this time I was being educated. I was taught to count with my feet, to pick out numbers and colors, and to know the difference between men, women, boys and girls. I learned to add numbers together, to say Yes and No, to kiss my master, sit on a chair, even on his lap, without hurting him, make change on a cash register, play tunes on the chimes, and lots of other things.

My master was always good and kind to me while teaching me. He never got impatient, and he would stop every once in a while and let me rest, and he always gave me something nice to eat when I did well. So I used to look out of the window of my stable and see other horses dragging heavy loads, sometimes being driven fast by delivery-boys, in hot weather, until they were dripping with perspiration, or in winter-time, out in the snow or where the streets were so slippery that they fell down. I often heard their drivers shouting roughly at them and using foul language, and I have seen them whip their poor animals cruelly, and then I knew how much better off I was than they, and it made me feel very thankful and grateful to my good master.

He always talked nicely while he was training me; told me that if I was good and learned my lessons, people would come to see me, and they would love me, and he and my mistress and Chili would be very proud of me. He told me about some of the boys and girls who went to school, but who refused to learn their lessons, and the misery and wretchedness that often came to them as the result. So I grew more and more anxious to learn, for although I was only a horse, I wanted people to love me and think well of me, and say nice things about me.

For *five whole years* my master kept me at school. Every day he came to my stable, or took me out into the yard, to give me my lessons. I guess I was a slow learner, and it took a great deal of patience to make me remember, for I was only a horse—not a boy or a girl, with human intelligence. We had to go over the same lessons scores, hundreds of times, until I knew them by heart. But my master was kind all the time, seldom spoke angrily to me, and never whipped me, though he kept a small switch in his hand with which he gave me a gentle reminder, once in a while, when I was inclined to be a little more frolicsome than usual.

One day he came to me and said: "Now, Captain, you and I are going to travel and see the world. Do you know what I have been educating you for? I am going to let people all over this country see you, and what you can do, so that they will no longer be able truthfully to say that a horse has no intelligence. Chili will go along with us. When we are on the trains he will remain in your stall and travel with you, and when we stop anywhere to 'show' he will spend his nights with you as he has done all the time."

Just think what news this was for a horse! How I pricked up my ears! How I looked forward for the day to come when we should start!

At last the eventful day arrived. Quite a number of people came to see us go. Chili led me from my stable to what he called a box-car at the railway station. It had padded ends and sides so that, when the train bumped while the cars were being switched, or at the starting or stopping of the train, I could not get hurt. I am free to confess I didn't like the idea of going into the car at first and both my master and Chili had to persuade me before I went in.

When the train started I didn't like it at all, and I was uneasy for a few days whenever we were on the train, but Chili was always there, and he kept telling me there was nothing to be afraid of, so as I had learned to trust him, I soon stopped worrying, and *I have never worried since*. Some people tell me that in that regard I learned to be wiser than a great many humans, who ought to know that worrying does no good and yet they still go on doing it. How I pity such people that they don't have a little bit of simple *horse-sense*.

By and by I learned, as we traveled, to look out of the window and see what there was outside. What a lot of wonderful things I saw. Of course we kept stopping, sometimes for a week, then for only a day or two, and we gave exhibitions all the time, the people coming in large numbers to see me. They all wondered how my good master had succeeded in training and educating me so well. Then sometimes they came up and petted me, and the girls and women, and even the boys and men, kissed me on the nose, and said such nice and flattering things to me. I enjoyed it ever so much, for I like people to like me. And of course, my master never forgot to give me a carrot, or an apple, or a cookie, when I did well, so that he said I grew "fatter and saucier every day."

My very first public appearance and performance was in the lobby of the Sherman House, in Chicago, in August, 1913, at the Engineers' Convention. I went from there to the Great Northern Hippodrome, where I stayed for a whole week. Then we started and took the complete circuit of the Miles Theaters, starting from Chicago and going to New York one way, and returning to Chicago another way. I enjoyed it very much, and made lots of friends on that first trip.

When we got back to Chicago it was late in the fall of 1914, and my master told me we were not going to work any more publicly for several months, as he wanted to get me ready for the Panama-Pacific International Exposition at San Francisco, that was to open on the 20th of February, 1915. That great big long name made me nervous at first—I wondered what it meant. But by listening to my master and Chili talking I soon learned that it was a great and wonderful "show," in honor of the completing of the Panama Canal that united the Atlantic and the Pacific Oceans, and they called it "International" because all the nations of the earth were invited to take part in it.

Later I learned that there were to be magnificent buildings, bigger than any I had ever seen, even in Chicago and New York, Palaces of Music, and Education, and Fine Arts, and Mining, and Domestic Industries, and

Foreign Industries, of Liberal Arts, and Electricity, and Engineering, and Food Products, and that, besides, all the countries that took part, would have their own buildings. Then there were to be magnificent courts and fountains and arches and columns and domes and statues and bas-reliefs and pools and flower-gardens and trees, and at night-time searchlights and fireworks, and steam-works and illuminations more beautiful than anything of the kind men had ever seen before. So, even though I was only a horse, I was anxious to go and see it all.

Then Chili told me there was to be one whole long street devoted to pleasures and amusements, that they were to call the ZONE, and we were to appear there. There was to be a wonderful exhibit showing the appearance and working of the Panama Canal, villages of strange people from all over the world, Cowboy shows, Mining Camps, a representation of the seven days of Creation, and the Battle of Gettysburg, Capt. Scott's Trip to the South Pole, the fight of the Dreadnoughts and Submarines, an Incubator for babies—human babies, mind, the tiniest little humans you ever saw,—the Grand Canyon, the Pueblo Indian village, the Yellowstone National Park, the Streets of Cairo, Toyland, the Japanese town, and lots of others that I do not now recall. We were to have our show right on the Zone, and be one of these many marvelous and wonderful attractions. The more I heard about these things the more anxious I was to go, and yet I wondered a good deal as to whether I should be as attractive to the crowd among so many other interesting things as I had been where there were not so many. But my master and Chili seemed satisfied, so I stuck to my motto and "Quit Worrying."

Day after day we rehearsed my performance and went over my lessons, until my master said I was "sure perfect." That made me feel good. Then one day I heard master tell Chili to go and see that his orders were carried out about the car, and I learned then that the car was ordered that was to take me to San Francisco, and that the workmen were busy at work upon it, padding it and making it comfortable for me as well as Chili. When everything was ready and lots of hay and grain put in the car, Chili took me aboard, and that night we started. Over the plains of Illinois and Iowa, into Nebraska and Wyoming, through Utah and Nevada we rode. What a lot of different country I saw from any I had ever seen before. When we reached the mountains I thought they were wonderful, and how I enjoyed the ride, as we raced down from Summit to Cheyenne. At Reno we began the climb over the Sierras and Chili said we were in California. I had heard it was a land of sunshine and flowers and birds and fruit, but we were in a region of rocks and mountains, precipices and canyons, snow and ice, and while there were plenty of beautiful trees I couldn't see a single flower. When Chili brought, from one of the streams, several times a day, a bucket of water for me to drink, it was colder than any well-water I had ever been given in my life. My! how it made my teeth ache. But it was so sweet and tasted so good, as if the winds of God had blown over it for months, bringing freshness and sweetness and filling it full of their deliciousness.

As soon as we reached the summit we began to go down, down, down, to lower levels, and long before we left the snow I could smell the sweet growing timothy and clover and alfalfa, and even the blossoms on the fruit-trees, and when we reached Auburn and Newcastle and lots of other towns up there, we were in the real California I had always pictured. Larks and thrushes, linnets and mocking-birds, song-sparrows and warblers were there by the thousands, singing such songs as I had never heard, and flowers! There were flowers of a thousand kinds, all new to me, pushing their way up through the green grass; and as for the fruit-trees, although it was early in February, there were thousands of them already in bloom and as sweet and fragrant and beautiful as a Garden of Eden.

It was the fourteenth of February, 1915, when we reached San Francisco. There Chili took me to a comfortable livery barn, where I remained until March 17. This was owing to the fact that the theater my master was having built for our performances, was not completed until that time. At the rear of it was a fine barn and stable for my use, where Chili could also sleep.

Though we began a month late we soon made up for lost time. The people came by the hundreds and then by the thousands. They petted me, and laughed at my tricks, especially when I felt good and came running onto the platform, kicking up my heels and having a general good time. The women called me a "dear," and a "darling," and the men said I was "remarkable," "a marvel," and "a wonder," and the boys said I was "a corker," and "a jim-dandy." Anyhow those who saw me pick out the good-looking ladies, and the fine-looking men, sort out colors, add, subtract, multiply, give change on the cash register, pump, corkscrew, hobby-horse, sit on my master's lap, play the chimes and do my various exhibitions of thought, memory and reason, went away and spread my fame. My master, of course, felt very happy over it, for each day the receipts grew larger. But, as more people came, I had to give performances more often, and I soon began to think I was overworked. My master didn't think so, but he didn't realize how tired I got. I tried to tell him, as well as I knew how, but he didn't seem to pay any attention, and I was beginning to feel that he loved money better than he loved me. But all this time he was watching me very closely, and one day, when I was quite tired, he did not let me give so many performances. Then, too, there was another thing that was bothering me. While I loved Chili very dearly, as he was always good to me, somehow he was not so careful and attentive to my needs in San Francisco as he had been hitherto. I began to watch him and found he came in late, very often, and I soon saw that he was getting into bad company. As soon as my master found this out, he let him go, and secured for me a new groom. He is a "cullud genman,"—a real negro gentleman, from the South, who thoroughly understands fine horses, and whose name is Jasper, and we soon became very much attached to each other.

Just about this time a beautiful little woman came right up to my stall and said, as she gave me some sugar: "You beautiful creature. I've been watching your performance. You are wonderful. I'm afraid they're working you too hard. You should have some one to help you. I'm going to ask Captain Sigsbee if he won't let me come and relieve you."

I pricked up my ears at this and watched and listened very intently when she went to my master. I then learned that her name was Madame Ellis, and she said she was a mind-reader and telepathist. She explained that she had watched me give the blindfold part of my entertainment with the greatest interest, and was well satisfied that I understood every word that was said to me. Then came the words that almost made me dance for joy, for she said: "Captain Sigsbee, I give a blindfold entertainment that would go wonderfully well with your Captain's exhibition, and at the same time give him plenty of opportunity to rest and take a good breathing spell between performances."

My good master seemed as pleased as I was, for he immediately made the arrangement with Mr. Ellis, and the very next day Madame Ellis appeared on my platform. No one will ever know how much I was interested at this first performance of hers. I watched her every move, for when they wanted me to go to my stable and rest while she performed, I clearly showed them I did not want or intend to go. I stood and saw the whole performance, and I can only say that if Madame Ellis is as pleased with what I do, as I am with what she does, then she is a very pleased woman.

We became the best and dearest of friends and have so remained ever since, for when a horse gives his friendship he is not like some human beings I have seen, fickle and faithless, but is constant and faithful. We have never had the sign of a quarrel, and there is not the slightest jealousy between us. She is as proud of my triumphs and success as I am of hers. And they tell me that as far as earning money is concerned Madame Ellis and I earned more than any other show on the Zone, not even excepting the wonderful Panama Canal and the picture of Stella.

There were a great many very noted people came to see us while we were in San Francisco. Mr. C. C. Moore, president of the Exposition, and Mrs. Moore, together with Mayor and Mrs. Rolfe, and thousands of others from all over the world, as well as those who lived in San Francisco became my good friends. After I had gone away President Moore wrote the following letter to my master, which I am proud to have people read:

PANAMA-PACIFIC INTERNATIONAL EXPOSITION,
1915

San Francisco, California

OFFICE OF THE PRESIDENT

Oct. 6, 1916.

CAPTAIN W. A. SIGSBEE.

Dear Sir: It is a pleasure to me to inform you how much I enjoyed the performance of your horse "Captain" at the Panama-Pacific International Exposition, which I saw a number of times. The performance of this highly intelligent animal was a great attraction to visitors to the Exposition.

Very truly yours,

CHAS. C. MOORE, *President*.

When the Exposition closed in San Francisco, my master and Jasper took me down to Venice, in Southern California, where we stayed until March 18, 1916, when we moved to the Panama-California International Exposition at San Diego. Of course, there was nothing like the large number of people here that there were in San Francisco, but we made many good friends and had some large audiences. Among those I esteem most highly were President and Mrs. G. Aubrey Davidson and their children; Mr. H. J. Penfold, the secretary, and all the officials. They all used to come and pet me whenever opportunity arose, and many of the leading men and women of the city seemed glad to call themselves my friend. But I am free to confess that I have a few very special friends, and one of these is the great singer, Ellen Beach Yaw. While singing in the San Francisco Exposition she used to come to see me often, and became much attached to me, as I to her, and both there and in San Diego she would sing to me. Some people think I don't understand music, in spite of my playing accurately different tunes on the chimes, but my master and Jasper both know that when I am nervous and tired, on the other hand, frolicsome and frisky, I am always glad to stand with perfect quietude and restfulness when my dear Miss Yaw comes to sing to me. As soon as she holds up her hand and looks at me I know she is going to pour out a sweet song that will delight me, so I listen with all my attention. And she never has to wait for my appreciation. I go right up to her and kiss her my thanks for her song as soon as she has done singing.

Another thing I enjoy amazingly. Quite as well as I like music, I like to go out and stand in the sun. I think one of my far-away ancestors must have lived in, and loved, a desert country where the sun shone all the time, for I am never so happy as when Jasper allows me to go out and stand where the beams of the sun come straight down upon my back. It feels so good, and it soothes me so that I like to enjoy it and go to sleep enjoying it. And if they would allow me to, I would go out and roll in the sunshine, and then lie down, as a cat does before the fire, reveling in the warmth and going to sleep under its influence.

Sometimes people wonder how I make my wants known, seeing that I can't speak. With my master and Jasper I seldom have any trouble, for by pawing or whinneying I arrest their attention, and then there are many things I need that they quickly ask about. If they think I want water, they ask: "Water?" If I want it, I nod; if not, I shake my head. And so with going out, untying me, giving me more air—for I like plenty of fresh air—or anything else I may desire.

There are some people who think I don't like to give performances. I'm sure I don't know why, except that I do get tired a little once in a while, and sometimes my master wants me to be quiet and good when I feel frisky and frolicsome and want to kick up my heels. I always feel better the busier I am, and I remember one day in San Francisco, when we gave nineteen performances, I was so full of fun and spirits when we got through that Jasper had to be pretty stern with me before I would quieten down.

Another thing that amuses me. People often ask if I ever eat anything besides oats and hay, and things of that kind. It amuses me because I like everything, just as most healthy boys and girls do. I eat bread and butter—and I like it with jam on or sugar or honey—and hard boiled eggs, and nuts, and every kind of fruit, raw, cooked or preserved. Candies I just dote on, and vegetables come as a welcome change. I can eat them raw or cooked, hot or cold, and I don't object to lettuce put in sandwiches.

Sandwiches? Of course I eat them: ham, beef, chicken or tongue, with mustard or without. And nothing I like better, at times, than a ham bone to gnaw on. Sometimes Prince—Jasper's pet dog—brings one in and shares it with me, and I enjoy it amazingly.

But one of my special delicacies is cake. My dear mistress, Mrs. Sigsbee, long ago found that out, and whenever she wants to make me feel extra good she makes a cake for me. My! My! She is a fine cake-maker. One day she had made a large cake for a party. I think it was Master's birthday, and they had invited a lot of friends. That day Master loosed me from the stable and sent me up to the house to see Mistress. Sometimes he does this, and trusts me to go directly there. I did so this time, and when I got into the yard I went right to the kitchen window, which was open, and through which a delicious odor came. Right there on the table was the cake. It was this that smelled so good. I put my nose close to it and it made my mouth water. There was no one there to tell me not to do it, so I just bit right into the middle of it, took a large mouthful, and it—what do the boys say— "went to the right spot." The trouble was that first mouthful whetted my appetite for more, and I had made a pretty big hole in that cake before Mistress came in and found what I had done. She drove me away, but began to laugh so heartily that when Master came running, in answer to her call, she could scarcely speak. She could just point to the cake and to me. There I was, with cake crumbs and jam or jelly all over my nose and in my whiskers, and Mistress at last managed to gasp out, between laughs, "Captain's celebrating your birthday. He likes cake, too!"

At first Master was inclined to be mad, but Mistress laughed him out of it, and said why shouldn't I like birthday cake as well as he. She'd make another, and even if she couldn't, she would buy one. Then she put the rest of the cake away, and every day for another week I had a chance again to celebrate Master's birthday.

Do I ever get ugly-tempered?

I think I can truthfully answer that I do not show temper very often. I must confess, however, that now and again I am not as well-dispositioned as I generally am. Sometimes I feel a little out of sorts, and then I act up just as a naughty boy or girl does. I want my Master to hurry up my performance and let me get away, and I bungle and stumble and do the very thing I ought not to do. When I feel like this and have to pick out the colors, I grab the cloth viciously, and sometimes deliberately take the wrong one, or slam the drawer of the cash-register, and when it comes to playing the chimes it is too funny the way I find myself acting. When I reach the last few notes I hit them one after another as fast as I can, and then run around the stage to show Master I am impatient to get away. I suppose boys and girls get that way in school sometimes. Anyhow that is what Master and some of the people who come to see me say, and I can well believe it, for there is not so much difference between my actions and those of boys and girls, if people could only understand them aright.

One day Jasper brought a pigeon into the stable. I heard him say a lady had given it to him. We soon became the best of friends. The pigeon would coo to me and come onto my feeding rack, and I would nuzzle up to her and whinney. She flies about me and lights on my head and struts up and down my neck and back, and I just enjoy it. We often go to sleep together, I with my head close up against the pigeon, she snuggling close to my soft nose. I feel so much better now that I have so nice a companion. I am not so nervous when I hear strange footsteps, or just before we are going to have a show.

Sometimes I am so full of fun and frolic that my Master lets me play awhile. Then I just enjoy running about the stage, kicking up my heels, showing my teeth at people, and making believe I am very savage, hitting a note on the chimes, and dashing across to the cash register, opening the drawer and ringing the bell, and then picking up a colored cloth in my teeth and shaking it as if I were angry. But as soon as I have had enough of this I quieted down, and we go ahead with a "show" as steadily as can be. You see, my Master understands me, and doesn't all the time feel that he has to hold me in to make me "behave"—as people call it. I'd like to know why I shouldn't have high spirits and be happy and jolly, if any horse on earth should. I'm well cared for day and night; I have all I want to eat of the very best that money can buy; I am housed in the most comfortable stable that can be hired, with plenty of good, clean bedding, and a rug to keep me warm at night; I have my companions, the pigeon, and Prince, the fox terrier, and Jasper is on hand all the time, so why shouldn't I be full of frolic. That comes from being happy and healthy, and any one with sense can see that I am both, for my eyes are clear, my breath is sweet, my skin is clean and I am full of life and spirits.

My Master is good to me and I love him very dearly, but I am free to confess I have a special affection for Madame Ellis's little girl. She is about ten years old, and we are real chums. Her name is Margaret. She comes nearly every day to see me, and she pets me, and I pet her. She brings me sugar and apples, and then after I have eaten them she sits on my back, and after a while we play circus. She takes her shoes off—so that she won't hurt me—and stands on me, walks from my shoulders to my tail, standing either looking frontwards or backwards, and I walk around carefully so as not to make her fall. And when we get through she hugs and kisses me, and I like it amazingly and kiss her back, and would hug her if I knew just how to do it.

And now I have told my story. Now that the San Diego Exposition is over my master, I expect, will take me all over the country, so that more people may see me and become interested in my education. He feels that the performances I give will interest children and those who have to handle horses and thus lead them to treat all horses with more respect and kindness. When human beings feel that horses have intelligence,—no matter how small in quantity, or good in quality it may be,—they will act differently towards them. It will lead them to be more tolerant, patient and kind.

We hope to work with all the Humane Associations and Societies for the Prevention of Cruelty to Animals, for my master knows, as I also well know, that when children and teamsters see me and watch what I can do, their hearts become more gentle towards all animals, and thus the day is hastened when kindness and love shall reign supreme upon the earth.

HOW I BOUGHT AND TRAINED CAPTAIN
By His Owner, W. A. SIGSBEE

(*EDITOR'S INTRODUCTION.* To render the story of Captain complete it was essential that the reader should know something of his trainer, his educator, the man to whose enthusiasm and ability we owe the pleasure the horse has afforded us. Consequently I have questioned Capt. Sigsbee, again and again, as to his methods and the story which here follows contains his answers to these many questionings which I have put into consecutive and readable form, but, as nearly as is possible, in his own words.)

I was brought up in the horse business. My father and uncles were horsemen before I was born. They lived in Dane County, Wisconsin, twelve miles from Madison, and there I first saw the light. One of my uncles had trotting horses, and almost as soon as I could do anything I used to go and help him. When I was fourteen years old I was regularly employed by him during my vacations, to help on the farm, in the stables, and to accompany him to the trotting track. I soon learned to ride, as a jockey, and up to the time I was eighteen years old that was my occupation. Then I began to work for myself. I bought, educated or trained, and then sold horses and dogs. I was much interested in them, and always seemed to have fair success in their management.

As I grew older I used to go with my own horses to the County and State Fairs, the latter being held at Madison. When I was twenty-four years old I married, settled down on a farm, and as horse-trading seemed to be the business I was especially adapted for, naturally I followed it. Whenever my neighbors wanted a horse that was extra well trained they would come to me, and if I showed them one that could do a few tricks, they liked it none the less, and were not unwilling to pay a little extra for the pains I had taken.

The year after I was married I moved to Humboldt, Iowa, where I bought another farm and for four more years continued my work as farmer and horse-trader. Then I bought the Park Hotel, in the town of Humboldt, which I ran for eleven years, never, however, for one moment losing my interest in horses. In fact, it was one of the most profitable parts of my business. Many farmers, show-men, circus-men and others came to the town and stopped at my hotel, so I was never away from the atmosphere of the horse ring. Many a time, when they were in a tight place, the show or circus men would come and ask me to help them out, for my reputation as a trainer had spread, and it was pretty generally understood that I was an exceptional hand for teaching horses and dogs rather unusual and interesting tricks.

In time the great circus-masters, like Barnum and Bailey, Al Ringland and others, came to me and asked me to train horses for them, so that my horse business grew, and with it my reputation. Naturally I was always on the look out for colts that promised well, or horses that seemed extra intelligent, and my eyes were keen for mares that showed a superior order of intelligence that were soon to have colts.

About this time my eyes were attracted to a beautiful mare, evidently with foal. No sooner did I see her than I wanted her. I found on inquiry that she had been bred to a spotted Arabian, as fine and beautiful a creature as she herself was. Satisfied that she was what I wanted, I purchased her. Already I had begun to speculate as to what I should do with her colt. If it was a prettily shaped animal, was as intelligent as the father and mother, I decided it should receive the best education I was capable of giving. As the days of the mare's time passed I grew more and more anxious. My hopes were raised high, and I was correspondingly expectant and at the same time afraid. What if the colt should prove stupid? I awaited the birth of that colt as eagerly as a royal family awaits the birth of the child of a king, hence you can understand my delight and satisfaction, when the little lady came, that I found her faultless in appearance, neat, trim, dainty and beautiful, with intelligent eyes and face and every indication of being a most superior animal.

From the hour of her birth I watched her far more closely than many a child is watched. I was in and out of the stable a score of times a day. While she appeared intelligent, I wanted to know with certainty as soon as I could. I was not long in discovering, and this was how it was done. My barn had double doors—one on each side. As it was warm weather I had both doors open to allow a current of air through the building. When the colt was four or five days old, I wished to hitch up the mare and drive her, but did not think it wise to let so small and young a colt go along. So I closed the doors and left her inside. She became much excited at being separated from her mother; ran around wildly, whinnied, and generally fretted. But I felt she would have to learn to lose her mother, so I drove away and left her to fight it out as best she could.

The next day I went into the barn and groomed down the mare, the colt apparently paying no attention, but the moment I took the harness from its peg and began to put it upon the mother the little miss ran out of doors. I thought I had scared her in some way and paid no particular attention, but when I was ready to drive away and tried to get her back into the barn she positively refused to go or be driven. She was as resolved to stay out as I was to have her go in, and it was only when I secured additional help that I was able to get her inside.

The same thing occurred on the following day, and then I began to suspect that the colt knew as well as I did what was going on, and was resolved not to be left behind. So I called to my wife to come and watch with me, while we experimented. So long as I merely fussed around with the mare, cleaning her, etc., it was all right, but the moment I touched the harness and made it appear I was going to hitch up, out shot the colt from the barn in a moment. We tried this out a dozen times and always with the same result. This occurred when she was nine days old, and with conviction I turned to my wife and exclaimed: "She'll do, the little Trixy; she's got brains, and I'll begin to train her right away." Thus she got her name, and I started upon her education.

In my past experience I had taught many horses to respond to questions with a Yes or No, to paw out numbers, to kiss me, to sit down, lie down, roll over, and other similar simple tricks. I would ask if they would like a drink, a feed of oats, a lump of sugar, etc., and teach them how to answer with a nod of the head, and with a shake when I asked: "Shall I whip you?" or "I guess you don't want any feed today," but with Trixey I determined to go further than this and see if she really could be trained, or, better still, *educated* in any degree.

Thus began Trixey's education, which continued persistently for eighteen months. Every day I kept at it, and it might be interesting here to state that while I was educating Trixey, she was educating me. I learned a great deal about horses and horse nature in those eighteen months. In due time I had trained her so that she could pick out numbers on call, colors, could add, subtract, multiply and divide; could count with her feet, sit in a chair, on my lap, and answer questions.

I then decided to take her out on the road and give exhibitions with her. But first of all I decided to give a test exhibition at our County Fair, at Humboldt, my own town. Of course I was well known, and my horse-training proclivities were the subject of conversation all throughout the country, but few knew how much I had accomplished with Trixey. Hence that first appearance was a great surprise to my neighbors. Needless to say, it was also a wonderful success. Every one was delighted with the exhibition and marveled at the intelligence the beautiful little creature displayed.

I now started to go throughout the country with confidence. I knew what Trixey could do and what the effect of the exhibition would be upon an audience. In those days an educated horse was unknown. There were a few trained circus horses, but a horse like mine excited great wonder and interest. My method was to go to County and other Fairs, explain what Trixey could do, and I would undertake to exhibit her before the grand stand between races. The Fair Associations would engage me, and thus I would earn a good financial return.

Soon after we began to travel I changed the colt's name to *Princess Trixey*, and this was the name by which she was ever afterwards known. About this time I came in contact with William Harrison Barnes, of Sioux City. He had been a newspaper reporter, but was naturally a showman, and shortly before I met him he had drifted into the show business. He was exhibiting such horses as "The Pacing Wonder," "Johnny, the Guideless Wonder," and when he saw the Princess there was nothing for it but that he should become my partner and go along with us. For four years we traveled together, Barnes making the business arrangements for our appearance at Carnivals, State Fairs, Amusement Parks, and under the auspices of various organizations. Then I sold Princess Trixey to him, continuing to travel with him for four years, after which I returned to Humboldt, bought another farm and for two or three years did a little desultory training of horses, as before.

Let me here, in parenthesis, tell of Princess Trixey's unfortunate end. Barnes showed her all over the country to the great delight of all who ever saw her, until about ten years ago, when she was killed in a railway wreck at Baltimore.

Soon after my return to Humboldt I was urged by Dode Fisk, of Wonewoc, Wis., to plan and organize for him a show of trained horses, dogs, monkeys, etc., with a one-ringed circus. I did so, doing all the training of the animals myself. When we were ready to travel we had a sixteen-wagon show and I was appointed the arenic director. For four years I occupied this position, helping build up the show all the time, and at the end of three years we ceased traveling in wagons and became an eleven-car railway show. It was my regular duty to keep the animals in good condition, see that they were healthy and kept up to their work, and to train any new stock we might buy.

Four years of this life tired my wife, and she expressed the desire to get away from a large show. She wanted a rest at home, she said, and then, if I desired to travel she suggested I buy a young horse or a colt, train or educate it, and we would travel with that, without all the hard work, flurry and daily excitement attendant upon a large show.

In the main I agreed with my wife and, anyhow, I felt that she ought to be considered as much as myself, so I began looking out for such a horse as

I had in mind. I wanted another Trixey or, better, but scarcely hoped to find one very soon, or very easily. I was nearer to the end of my search, however, than I supposed, for almost immediately I heard of just such a colt as I was looking for at Oregon, Ill. Right away I went to see him, and there, to my unspeakable delight, I found Captain. His owner was Judge Cartwright, a great lover of and breeder of good horses. Captain was of standard bred trotting stock, and was half brother to the famous Sydney Dillon. His sire was the well-known horse Syed and his dam was the almost equally well known Robey. At first sight he pleased me immensely, and I sought to gain all the information possible about him. I learned that as a colt he was very friendly and playful, showing keen intelligence. He also possessed great speed, sometimes pacing in the pasture as fast as his mother could run. This had led his owner, as soon as he was two years old, to train him for ninety days for the development of speed, so that he was able to step his mile in 2:16. He undoubtedly would have made a fast pacing horse with further training. But fate had another destiny in store for him. I resolved to buy him. Naturally Judge Cartwright hated to part with so promising an animal, but I candidly laid my heart's desire before him. I showed him the influence it would have upon the rising generation if I could demonstrate that animals can reason, that they are capable of thought. Then I expatiated upon the easier life Captain himself would live than if he were to become a regular race-horse, and I appealed to the feeling of pride he—the judge—would possess were I successful—as I knew I should be—at having introduced so world-famous a horse as Captain would become, that he had bred and reared. And, finally, to clinch the matter, I produced a certified check for a thousand dollars, which I placed in his hand.

Thus the purchase was made, with the express understanding that Judge Cartwright should always be given the credit for the raising of Captain.

Perhaps here I ought to state that the colt's name up to this time had been Sid Bell. As I felt my whole future life's work and fame were going to center on this beautiful, young and intelligent creature, I renamed him, calling him by the name by which I was known to all my professional associates, Captain Sigsbee.

It was not long before we became intimately acquainted. He was a handsome fellow, a dappled chestnut, fifteen and one-half hands high, with broad forehead, large, intelligent eyes, well-shaped ears, deep, sensitive nostrils, mobile mouth, strong nose, a most pleasing face, and perfectly formed in every way.

I was satisfied from the first that in Captain I had a great subject for education. Already I began to plan what I would teach him. I was assured I could go far beyond anything I had hitherto done, even with the clever Trixey. One day in conversation with a group of horsemen, among whom was A1 Ringland, the great circus master, I stated some of my expectations. Ringland laughed at me, especially when I declared my intention of so educating a horse that he could do things blindfolded. He freely declared that he had no faith in horse education. He believed that horses could be trained only under the whip and spur. Said he: "I know you've done some wonderful things with Trixey, but animals are animals, and I don't believe that you can *educate* them. Let me give you some advice. Don't waste your time. Many a man has gone crazy by allowing a fool idea like this of yours to take possession of him."

I defended my ideas, however, and argued that my years of study of the horse had revealed things of horse-nature and character few even dreamed of. I was sure they could think and reason. Everybody knew that they had memory, and I was satisfied that I could educate this, or any other intelligent horse, to use his reason, no matter how small it was—in other words to think.

Ringland listened with interest, but made no pretense to hide his doubts, and again said I was going crazy when I affirmed my positive conviction that I could, and would, train Captain to take and obey orders *blindfolded*. He was certain it never could be done.

How well I have succeeded the hundreds of thousands who have seen Captain can best tell. It may also be interesting to recount Mr. Ringland's expressions when he saw Captain sometime after I began to give exhibitions with him. He said: "I confess myself beaten, Sigsbee, I take off my hat to you. What you have accomplished will be a revelation to the world, as it has been to me. In spite of my years of association with horses I never dreamed they had such powers in them. You have opened my eyes, and as others begin to see they will treat their animals with greater consideration, they will think more favorably of them, and no longer treat them as if they were mere brute instruments of their will or pleasure, without feeling or intelligence."

Mr. Ringland well stated what it has been one of my constant endeavors to bring about. I have always loved horses. I wanted to see them better treated, and it is with great satisfaction that I am learning every day that my exhibitions with Princess Trixey and now with Captain are bearing this kind of fruit.

When my purchase of the colt was completed, I took him to my training barn in Chicago and there began his education. The first thing to do was to get well acquainted and gain his affection. This was done by giving him plenty to eat, the best of care, speaking gently and kindly to him, petting him, and giving him dainties now and again, such as carrots, apples and sugar. My friends and acquaintances often laughed at me, and said I should never accomplish what I was after, but I persevered. They knew I was wasting time, money and energy for nothing, but "I know" that what "they knew" wasn't so.

It did not take Captain long to learn that I was kind to him; that I was his true and wise friend; and was to be relied upon. These are three things, the importance of which I cannot over-estimate. Many people try to be kind to animals, but they are not wise in their treatment, and they are not to be relied upon. I knew that Captain trusted me for the little extra dainties he enjoyed. I never disappointed him. I never lied to him—that is promised him anything I did not intend to perform, and thus he soon learned I was to be trusted.

When left alone he became very uneasy. Like children he wanted companionship of some kind, so I hired a groom, Chili by name, whose duty was to remain with Captain, day and night. He was never to attempt to teach the horse anything, as that would lead to confusion, but was to care for him and be his companion at all times. Chili remained with him for several years and they became very fond of each other. I should never have parted with him, but when we came to San Francisco, he got careless and I had to let him go. Then I was fortunate enough to secure an equally good man in his present groom, Jasper. Jasper is a natural-born horseman. He has ridden, broken, and owned some very famous horses, and has been on the track for years, hence he thoroughly understands horse-nature, and he and Captain get along famously.

As I have before explained Captain likes company. He strongly resents being left alone. Every night-time before he goes to sleep he listens for the footsteps of his groom and if he is not there he signifies his disapproval by pawing, whinneying, etc., and generally keeps it up until Jasper returns and talks to him. Then, content and restful, he goes to sleep.

Once, when he was being brought south by rail, Jasper had to leave him in the Los Angeles freight yards—still in his car—to see that their tickets were properly endorsed, and he was gone for a half an hour or more. When he returned poor Captain was in a complete lather of perspiration. The unusual noises of the railroad yard in a large city, as he was shut up in a car so that he could not see, had fretted him into a frenzy. As soon as the groom returned he signified his satisfaction with whinneyings and nose-rubbings and in a very short time was cool again.

Every night before he lies down and goes to sleep, he peeks out to see if Jasper is there. If not, he awaits his return, and then stretches out with his head towards the place where Jasper sleeps.

Soon after we arrived in San Diego a lady presented Jasper with a pigeon. The bird was taken to the stable, and Captain became much interested in her. As the pigeon perched on the partition he reached up and nuzzled it in the most affectionate manner. Not only did the pigeon not resent it, but she seemed actually to enjoy it, showing no fear or desire to get away. Now they are almost inseparable friends, and Captain spends hours with his head upon the partition, snuggling close up to the bird. Prior to its coming, Captain often showed considerable nervousness when he heard strange footsteps approaching his stable, or just before a performance, but the presence of the pigeon has changed this. Its mere presence is a soothing influence, and when the show is over he goes back to the stable and greets his bird friend with evident pleasure and affection.

One of my experiences with Captain demonstrated his superior intelligence over most horses. My training barn was two stories high, and a wide pair of stairs led from the ground to the second floor. When my grandson was born Captain took a great liking for him. He loved to "kiss" him and nuzzle him while he was in the cradle, or baby-buggy, or even in his nurse's arms. As the child grew older we used to place him on Captain's back and Captain would march back and forth, as proudly as a king, apparently conscious of the trust we placed in him.

One day while I was working with Captain the child was in the barn, and he kept going up and down the stairs. I noticed that Captain's attention was more often fixed upon the child than upon me and he seemed much interested. Someone called me away for a few moments, and when I returned there was no Captain to be seen. Then I heard a peculiar noise from above, and looking up, what should I see but Captain following the child up the stairs. I am free to confess I got scared, for I couldn't see how I could get him down. But I went up, controlled my fears, and then quietly talked to Captain and told him he'd come up the stairs and now he'd have to go down them. And I backed him down, a step at a time, as easily and as safely as could be. And, strange to say, ever after that, whenever he wanted to go upstairs I let him, and he came down alone. I never had to back him down again. He comes down that way of his own volition.

People often ask me how I train an animal. Personally I would not use the word "train," in speaking of such a horse as Captain, not because it is the wrong word, but because it conveys a wrong idea. I would say "educate," for I firmly believe that horses and dogs and elephants and other animals possess the power of reason, though, of course, in a limited degree.

And I believe that by patient and kindly treatment we can "draw out,"—educate—the intelligence possessed.

I have no set rules or fixed system by which I work. There are a few principles that control me. First of all I study the animal's nature and disposition. No two animals are alike, any more than any two children are alike. Some animals are very nervous, are easily excited, while others are placid and docile and nothing seems to disturb them. But whatever the natural disposition nothing can be done without gaining the animal's complete confidence. This I do by uniformly kind treatment. I always speak gently, mildly, never angrily or impatiently. Then I pet the animal at every opportunity, though with some, one must approach them at first, cautiously. As soon as possible get an animal accustomed to the feel of your hands, and to know that they always come gently, and with soothing effect. Find out what they particularly like to eat, and every once in a while, give this to them as a relish, a luxury, a reward for something well done. As I have explained elsewhere horses like carrots, apples and sugar. Too much of any of these, however, is not good, as their natural food is grass, hay, cereals, and the like. Yet it should never be overlooked that a horse, like a man, can more easily be reached through his stomach than any other way.

Though you must be kind you must also be firm. Many people confound and confuse kindness with mushiness. No animal must be allowed to have his own way, when that way conflicts with his master's will. (Yet a caution, here, is necessary. One who is training either a horse or a child should remember his natural proclivities and tendencies. There should be no attempt to "break the will." It is to be trained, disciplined, brought under control. Hence, never set your will against the will of your animal unless it is in a matter where you know you are right.) For instance, if a horse wants to cut up and frolic when you wish him to attend to business, there are two ways of doing. One is to leave him alone for awhile and then firmly bring him to attention, even though he still desires to continue his fun. Another is to crush the spirit of fun and frolic and not allow him to play at all. This latter method is unnatural, unreasonable, and cruel, and therefore not to be thought of for one moment by any rational or kind man. The former is both kind and *disciplinary*. The horse is allowed to follow his natural instincts, but is also taught to control them at his master's word. This is training and education. A third method is to allow the horse to frolic to his heart's content and then get him to do what you desire. Here there is no discipline whatever. This is the way of "mushiness," and it is often followed by parents and others in handling their children. It is about as bad as the cruel method of suppressing the natural instincts, for an uncontrolled will or appetite soon becomes the child's, animal's, or man's master, and nothing is more disastrous than such a bondage.

Hence be firm in control. It is not necessary to whip to punish. A horse, as well as a child, will learn self-control through appetite, or the giving of something that is a pleasure. Where you have trouble in gaining control, or where the animal is lazy, hold back on the tidbit, or the free run, or something of the kind the horse enjoys. He will soon learn to associate the loss with his disobedience. Equally so be prompt and certain in rewarding his good conduct. It is a good thing in dealing with a stubborn or refractory animal (or child) to let him get "good and hungry." It does not take him long to learn to associate obedience with food, or disobedience with hunger.

Then it is most important that you never lie to an animal. Be strictly truthful. When you promise anything—or by forming a habit imply a promise—do not fail to keep that promise. If your animal expects an apple, a carrot, a piece of sugar or a frolic at the close of his hour's training, *do not disappoint him*. A horse, a child, instinctively hates a liar. One soon loses confidence, and where there is no confidence there can be no pleasure in working together, and as soon as pleasure goes, the work becomes a burden, a labor, a penalty, and a curse, to be dreaded, shunned, avoided. So win your animal's confidence and then be sure to keep it.

When it comes to actual teaching always be very patient, never excited, always talk gently and keep your voice pitched low, and remember that all animals are curious, possess more or less of the imitative faculty, and have good memories. To remember these things is of great importance. Never lose sight of them. Talk to your animal as you would to a child. Whether you think or believe he understands you, or not, act and talk as if he did. Then *show* him what you want him to do. Do it before him, again and again. Thus you will excite his imitative faculties and at the same time, train his memory.

Occasionally you may be able to give him extra aid. For instance, you want to teach your horse to shake his head to express the idea No! When you say No! tickle the horse's ear, and he will shake his head. Then you also shake your head, and say with emphasis, No! Repeat this several times, and you will find that when you say No! the horse will shake his head without your having to tickle his ear. As soon as he responds to your question with a shake of the head be sure to pet and reward him with a lump of sugar, at the same time talking encouragingly to him.

Then repeat the process, again and again, until it is well fixed in his memory.

Ellen Beach Yaw, "Lark Ellen" of California, Singing to Captain at the San Diego Exposition.

Captain awakening his groom by pulling off his bed clothes. This is a regular trick of Captain's, when Jasper fails to get up and give him his breakfast at the proper time.

Every day go over this same thing; for, if you neglect what he learns today for a week or two, it is very possible he will forget and you will have to begin afresh. Review perpetually, until you know that *he knows*.

In assisting him to nod his head when you want him to signify Yes! when you use the word tap him under the chin. This leads him to throw his head up and down. Soon he will nod at the mere saying of Yes! and later, he will respond with a nod when you ask him a question to which he should reply with the affirmative.

Remember always, in all you do, that you are dealing with an animal whose brain power is far less than that of an ordinary child, and be *patient*, *kind and persevering*. Never allow yourself to believe the animal does not possess intelligence. *Believe* he has it, *hope* he has it, *trust God* that he has it and work in that belief, hope, trust, and you will accomplish wonders. Faith, hope and love are the abiding and moving powers of life. With them there is no limit to what can be done, for they belong to the infinite.

A SCIENTIFIC INVESTIGATION

It is natural that, to those who are skeptical as to a horse's brain capacity, there should be some doubt as to the reality of Captain's performances. Suggestions of trickery, of Captain's being controlled by visual or aural cues that are unobserved and generally unobservable by the public, arise in the mind. The skeptic denies, positively and unquestionably, any assertion of the animal's intelligence. He laughs and scoffs at the idea that the horse really thinks, adds, subtracts, multiplies or counts; that he knows colors; that he has any idea whatever of tone values, or, indeed, can tell one note from another. He believes in suggestions, or cues, or even that, unconsciously, Mr. Sigsbee hypnotizes the horse and thus personally directs all his actions, and he does not seem to see that these involve the explanation of mysteries as deep as the one of animal intelligence.

The first thing, however, is to be assured that the horse actually does the things it is asserted he does, and that, as far as the trained and scientific observer can detect, there is no conscious deception. In the case of Captain this has been done by Dr. G. V. Hamilton, a veterinarian, whom the *Santa Barbara* (Calif.) *Press* asserts is "nationally recognized as an expert in these avenues of investigation." After witnessing a public performance he conducted a series of private tests and from the *Press* of February 27, 1916, I quote the following account from Dr. Hamilton's pen:

> Several days elapsed between the visit at which I took the notes recorded above and my private interview with Captain and Mr. Sigsbee. This enabled me to plan various tests which might enable me to check up on the following possibilities:
>
> In performances of this kind it is at least possible for a confederate to conceal himself behind the curtains, under the stage or elsewhere, and to direct the activities of the animal.
>
> A short whip or stick might easily carry a long, thin, black wire, which would be invisible from the front of the stage.
>
> My experience with laboratory animals leads me to believe that it would be possible for a shrewd animal trainer to direct a dog's or a horse's activities by means of eye, facial muscle and bodily movements which are of a too slight excursus to be apparent to ordinary human observation. It is not to be forgotten, in this connection, that some dogs are notoriously

dependent on their masters for directive cues, and that this may be characteristic of horses of a certain type.

It is conceivable that repetition of a given routine over a period of years might enable a horse to stereotype a highly complex set of habits.

On the morning of my appointment with Mr. Sigsbee I found the horse in his stall, unattended. A colored groom, who seems to be the only person, other than Mr. Sigsbee, to have any responsibility for Captain, shortly appeared. He discussed the horse with me without manifesting either suspiciousness or constraint. A little later Mr. Sigsbee came to the stall and asked me to decide how and where to make the tests. He seemed to be wholly unaware of the possibility that my tests might seriously impair the "show" value of his animal. I decided to work with the horse on the stage, and to have Mr. Sigsbee with me. Captain is a nervous, highly excitable animal, and I had previously seen him make a poor showing when not in good condition, hence my desire to have the familiar presence of the master.

A careful examination of the stage revealed no evidence of provision for the concealment of a confederate, so I had Captain led upon the stage and began my tests, which were given in the following order:

1. I asked him, "How do you walk when you go to see your girl?" Captain gave an appropriate response, although his master was not within the horse's field of vision, and did not carry his whip. Mr. Sigsbee who seems to have a great affection for his horse, now interpolated, "What do you give me for sugar?" Captain "kissed" him.

2. At my request Mr. Sigsbee asked Captain to play "Nearer My God to Thee." I stood between horse and master while the former played the chimes with but one mistake. He received no direction for this after the initial command. Mr. Sigsbee then told me that Captain knew how to run the scale, so I asked for that. The horse made one mistake, due to his failure to strike the trip hammer opposite one of the metal tubes with sufficient force. When he had passed from the low to the high end of the chimes his master commanded him to "come right back," and this was promptly obeyed. Still no visual cues. As a matter of fact, the horse seemed to pay almost no attention to Mr. Sigsbee

with its eyes, as it were, but kept its ears in almost constant movement.

3. The leather blindfold was now applied. There is not the slightest doubt in my mind as to the entire adequacy of Captain's blindfold for purposes of excluding visual stimuli. At my request Mr. Sigsbee stood facing me and called for 2, 9, 3, 1, and 7 separately and in the order given. The horse stood where I had previously decided to have him stand, and I made sure that no directive stimuli were reaching him either from the stage or from the rear and sides.

He stamped twice for "2," nine for "9," etc., until this test was completed. The only mistake occurred when, in response to the command to "give us three" he stamped three times and struck his toe on returning his foot to the standing position. His master accused him of this mistake and Captain gave us three clean-cut taps.

4. I gave the command, "Give me your right foot," "Give me your left foot," "Put your head down and bite your right knee," and "Scratch your head." He responded appropriately, although it was necessary for me to repeat these commands to satisfy the inquiry contained in Captain's wiggling ears. Mr. Sigsbee stood by my side, a wholly negligible factor for the moment. I am thoroughly satisfied that Captain's activities were solely directed by my commands.

5. Captain, still blindfolded, was given the following problems by his master, from whom I had concealed my program. It seemed to be difficult for the horse to follow my unfamiliar voice, and since Mr. Sigsbee was invisible to the horse and wholly under my control I decided to employ him as interlocutor:

"Divide ten equally between your two feet, the first half with your right foot, the second half with your left foot."

Captain stamped five times with his right foot, then pawed tentatively, apparently in doubt as to the correctness of his answer, and awaiting a cue. He received no cue, and soon withdrew his right foot to the standing position and tapped five times with the left foot. His master accused him of inaccuracy, telling him that he "got one too many" with his right foot. Captain corrected his mistake by giving us a clean-cut and accurate response.

"Divide twelve equally between your two feet, the first half with the right foot, the second half with your left foot."

This command elicited a perfect response.

"How much is three times three?"

A perfect response was again obtained. Captain gave nine taps with his right forefoot.

"How much is two times two?" I gave this command.

Captain tapped four times, stopped, and began to paw in a doubtful manner. His master scolded him for this, and he tried it again, but again at the end of four taps, hesitated and pawed. Mr. Sigbsee told him he knew better than that, and commanded him to try again. I gave the problem clearly, and obtained a correct and clean-cut response.

6. Mr. Sigsbee was instructed to give the following commands:

"Pump."

"Reverse."

"Laugh."

"Say 'Yes'."

"Wiggle your ears."

"Scratch your head."

"Stick out your tongue."

"Stretch out like a hobby horse."

I showed this list of written commands to Mr. Sigsbee, but instead of following my instructions he urged me to give them myself. It is still a source of surprise to me that this horse, while blindfolded and with no directive cues from his master (Mr. Sigsbee stood beside me and neither moved nor spoke), responded appropriately to these commands. It was necessary for me to repeat only one command—the last one.

7. At my direction Mr. Sigsbee tied the white strip of cloth to the blindfolded horse's left hind leg, and the red cloth to his right foreleg. At the end of this performance he cautioned Captain again and again not to forget that the "white rag is on your hind leg—here (patting the left hind leg), and the red rag is

on your foreleg." After much patting of both legs and many warnings against forgetting, Mr. Sigsbee withdrew and allowed me to decide upon the command. I called for the red strip, and Captain obeyed without displaying the least hesitation. It will be remembered that on a previous occasion he found the red strip on his hind leg.

8. The blindfold was now removed, and was not reapplied. Correct responses were obtained to the commands, "Bring me a silver dollar" and "Bring me a quarter." Mr. Sigsbee stood where it was impossible for him to direct Captain's choice by pointing with eyes, facial muscles or body.

9. I arranged the numerals in the number rack in the following order: 1, 2, 3, 4, 5, 6, 7, 8, 9, 0. Mr. Sigsbee stood behind the horse and gave the following command:

"How many people are there in the front row?"

Mrs. Hamilton was the only "audience" for the performance, and sat in the front row from the moment when Captain was brought upon the stage. The horse responded to the command by advancing to the railing over the footlights, extending his head and neck far forward and examining the front row of seats. He followed this by backing vigorously and pulling number "1" from the rack. In a flash of inspiration I asked, "How many people are there in the second row?" Captain walked forward again, looked into the second row and shook his head. I am glad that I have Mrs. Hamilton and my note book to remind me that this occurred when I was wide awake and in a very critical frame of mind. Mr. Sigsbee was standing to my left and the horse was to my right and several feet in front of us when this occurred. I expressed my unwillingness to believe my own senses, and Mr. Sigsbee quite seriously expressed the opinion that the horse had been influenced by the master's mind to shake his head.

10. I eliminated Mr. Sigsbee by placing him where I could keep my eye on him, but where he was outside the horse's field of vision. Then I commanded Captain to bring me number "6" from the rack. He obeyed and followed this by bringing me "4," "9," and "7."

11. I exchanged "1" and "4" and commanded Captain to tell me how many people were in the front row. He brought me number "1."

12. Mr. Sigsbee, at my direction, gave Captain the number, "30,724." The numbers in the rack were in the unfamiliar order, "1, 2, 3, 4, 5, 6, 7, 8, 9, 0." By obstructing Captain's view of his master I was able to eliminate the possibility of directing gaze-cues from master to horse. Long experience with my quadruple choice method has enabled me to control the movements of my ocular muscles, and to depend a good deal on peripheral vision, so that I am sure that I did not involuntarily direct the horse during this test.

Captain promptly pulled "3" from the rack, pulled "8" part way out and let go before he had fully withdrawn it, then withdrew "0," "7," "2," and "4" in rapid succession.

13. I put "4," "1," and "8" on the floor, sent Mr. Sigsbee to the rear of the stage and gave the following commands:

"Two times nine."

"Seven times twelve."

"Nine times nine."

The horse took up "1" and "8" in the response to the first command, and dropped them. I arranged the three numbers in the same order in which they lay on the floor before the first command was given ("4" was at the left end, "1" in the middle and "8" at the right end.) The second command was given, and answered correctly, without hesitation. I now reversed the positions of "4" and "8" and gave the third command, which was also answered correctly.

14. After I had rearranged the colored strips on the color rack so that black and white were near the middle (it will be remembered that they were end strips during the public performance), directed Mr. Sigsbee to command Captain to match Mrs. Hamilton's garments.

Captain went as far forward on the stage as he could go, craned his neck forward, and closely scrutinized Mrs. Hamilton. At the command, "Match the color of the lady's hat" (Mr. Sigsbee gave these commands), Captain went to the color rack, which was close to and near the middle of the right wing, and took the black strip in his teeth. (Correct.) His master stood behind him, facing Mrs. Hamilton, who sat in the first row as "audience." Following this the horse matched the white waist, tan gloves and black pocketbook.

I now engaged Mr. Sigsbee in a conversation as to how he had trained his horse to match colors, when Mrs. Hamilton called to Captain, "Can you match this?" Captain nodded his head and came up to the rack and took the yellow strip in his teeth. Neither Mr. Sigsbee nor I saw the pencil, and even when Mrs. Hamilton told us that it was a pencil I could not tell its colors from where Mr. Sigsbee and I stood, since the audience room was dimly lighted. On our way to the exposition that morning Mrs. Hamilton and I jested about my pencil-stealing proclivities, and I had reminded her that I had returned her red-white-and-blue pencil. This accounts for the certainty with which I declared that Captain had taken the wrong color until Mrs. Hamilton showed me that her pencil was really a yellow one.

Captain had grown friendly toward me, and as he stood facing me, apparently inviting attention, I said, "Match my necktie" and pointed to my red tie. He promptly pulled the red strip from the rack. Mr. Sigsbee was definitely behind Captain when this occurred.

Although my examination of Captain was too brief to justify me in presenting this as more than a preliminary report, there are a few tentative conclusions which I have drawn from it, and which I wish to present for the consideration of persons who may be interested in the training feats of men like von Osten, Krall, and Sigsbee.

1. The inquiring liveliness of Captain's ears and the freedom with which Mr. Sigsbee employs verbal directions when the horse is tired and inattentive suggests the possibility that this animal may receive auditory cues that are given involuntarily by his master. It is not only conceivable but even likely that Captain is sensitive to changes in his master's respiratory sounds. A spasmodic inspiration, a faint sigh or a sudden quickening of respiration might easily serve as cues for Captain. One need only translate Rendlich's and Pfungst's explanation of Hans' behavior from visual into auditory terms to arrive at a fairly satisfying guess as to how it is possible for Captain to perform his wonderful feats.

2. My observations, although incomplete and inconclusive in many respects, have convinced me that Captain can give correct answers in entire independence of directive visual stimuli. There was no trickery about his blindfold: Captain wore

a leather mask which so well excluded the light that he had to be led from place to place on the stage. Even when he was not blindfolded, and seemed to be keen to understand and to obey them correctly, he attended only with his ears.

3. I am convinced that Mr. Sigsbee is sincere in his belief that Captain is capable of abstract thought, and that he resorts to no trickery in his public performances. It is also gratifying to know that he is of the hard-headed type to whom a scientifically established explanation would be acceptable, even though it might run counter to his own presuppositions. If it proves to be the case that his horse is accessible to stimuli to which human ears are obtuse, and that master as well as public has been literally "taken in" by horse-cleverness the humorous aspect of the situation will appeal to him. From a purely commercial standpoint he need have no fear as to the "show" value of a horse which can beat a crafty old trainer at his own game by training the master to give such exquisitely delicate cues that the master himself is not aware of giving them. It is not surprising that Mr. Sigsbee had to fall back upon telepathic explanations.

CAPTAIN'S PRAYER OF THANKSGIVING

Prayer assumes two forms, the one of petition that blessings may be bestowed upon the petitioner, the other of thanksgiving for the blessings so bestowed. Several years ago a "Horse's Prayer" was published in the newspapers. It was a prayer of petition. But—presupposing the possession by the horse of intelligence and power to formulate prayer—Captain has never had to ask for most of the things set forth in this prayer. His kind master has freely accorded them to him, so Captain's prayer is one of thankfulness. But every owner of a horse can convert this prayer into one of petition by applying it to his own horse and seeing whether he is treating his animal as Captain is being treated:

> **My Dear Master, I thank thee for all thy goodness to me all the days of my life. Thou hast given me good, clean, nutritious food, plenty of water, perfect shelter, clean dry bedding, and a stall wide enough for me to lie down in with comfort. Every day my hair and skin have been brushed and cleaned, my nostrils washed out, and my mane and tail kept free from burrs, tangles and dirt.**
>
> You and the men you have employed to attend me have always been kind to me. You have talked gently to, and not shouted at, me. You have soothed me many times by the kind and assuring tones of your voice. When I have been nervous and afraid, instead of shouting at me, or whipping me, your gentle words have quieted and encouraged me. You have petted and caressed me and made me feel the joy of serving you because I love you. While you have been firm with me and made me do my work, you have never demanded more than I was able to give. You have never jerked my reins, and thus made my mouth sore, or cruelly whipped me as I have seen drivers do when their horses were pulling heavy loads up hill. You have always endeavored to explain what you have wanted me to do, and have not whipped, kicked, beaten, or cursed me when I did not understand. You have been kind in teaching me, gentle in bearing with my ignorance and mistakes, and patient when I have been slow to learn. When I did not obey you instantly, you have looked over my harness, my bridle, or my hoofs to see that nothing was amiss.

You have never checked up my head so that my neck was stiff and unable to move with freedom, and you have never cursed me with blinders that rubbed my eyelashes, were too close to my eyes, and that prevented me from looking behind me, as the great Creator intended I should do.

You have never overloaded, or overworked me; never hitched me where water could drop on me, or where I had to stand too long in the wet, and if it was cold weather you have always covered me with a blanket. My feet have always been well shod; you have always examined my teeth to see that they were kept in good condition, and never allowed "fox tails" to pierce my gums and make my mouth sore. You have never been so wicked and cruel as to cut away my tail so that I could not defend myself from flies and mosquitoes, and at night or day time, you have never tied my head up so tightly that it was in an unnatural position and prevented me from moving it easily, or lying down to sleep.

You have always seen that I had plenty of clean and cool water to drink, day and night, and you have watched me with care so that I should not get sick. While I love the warm sun you have not tied me where, when it was very hot, I could get no shelter. In winter time you have never allowed a frosty bit to be put in my mouth.

And though I am still young and healthy and apparently not likely to become feeble and useless for many years to come, the kindness you have already shown me assures me that when I do lose my strength and ability you will not turn me out into some poor pasture where I may starve or freeze, or sell me to some human brute who will whip and torture me to get the last fragment of work out of me, while he slowly starves me to death with poor and insufficient food. If it is impossible to put me where I shall have proper food and shelter I know you will mercifully, kindly, and swiftly take my life, and thus, even in the hour of death, I shall thank you with my whole heart.

And, though I am a horse, I am sure you have remembered that God is my Father and Creator as well as yours, or I should not be here, and that His Son said that

His Heavenly Father cared even for the sparrows, two of which were sold for a farthing, and that He himself ever sanctified a stable by the fact that He was born in one and cradled in the manger at Bethlehem. So, In His Name, I give you thanks for all your kindness to me, recalling to your memory His words that "inasmuch as ye have done it unto the least of these, my brethren, ye have done it unto Me."

—Amen.

Captain and a group of his admiring friends at the Panama-California International Exposition, San Diego. Captain W. A. Sigsbee (his owner and trainer) and President G. A. Davidson of the Exposition at his head.

Captain and George Wharton James with the pigeons at the San Diego Exposition, 1916.

Milton Keynes UK
Ingram Content Group UK Ltd.
UKHW042146281024
450365UK00010B/665